PAGES 2 LIFE **PUBLISHING**

R
L
W

Ministries

Business Consultant

Booklet Vol. #3

THE STRATEGY

EXAMINING THE PASSION & DRIVE OF A TRUE
Entrepreneur VOL. #3
&
EXHIBITING THE STAMINA & MENTALITY OF A GOOD
Businessman VOL. #4

© Copyright 2020 by **Roderick L. White** all rights reserved.

Printed in the United States of America. All inspirational references taken from the PURPOSED & DIVINE Trilogy Series © 2017, 2018, and 2019; and KING JAMES VERSION © 1987 presented on bible gateway, No part of this book may be used or reproduced in any manner whatsoever without written permission, except in the case of brief quotations embodied in critical articles and reviews. For more information, address Roderick L. White,

c/o rodwhitepastor1@icloud.com
www.RoderickLWhiteministries.com

ISBN: 9798579717191

Editor review: BookBaby & **RLW Ministries**
Editorial Layout & Formatting: PAGES 2 LIFE **PUBLISHING**

Library of Congress Cataloging-in-Publication Data:

An application to register this book for Cataloging has been submitted to the Library of Congress. Printed in the USA and Canada

Cover by **Spark Adobe**; book interior structure & pictorial design by, Pages 2 Life **Publishing**
Printed by, AMAZON

PUBLISHED BY
RODERICK L. WHITE MINISTRIES
Printed in USA by PAGES 2 LIFE **PUBLISHING**

Ministries
P.O. Box 10142
Jackson, TN. 38308
www.RoderickLWhiteministries.com

THE STRATEGY

Examining The **PASSION** & Drive Of A True Entrepreneur

PAGES 2 LIFE **PUBLISHING**

Ministries
Business Consultant
Booklet Vol. #3

THE STRATEGY

Examining the PASSION *& Drive Of A True Entrepreneur* VOL. #3

TABLE OF CONTENTS

STEP#1   Positivity produces good energy   pg. #5
Your mentality determines your level of success.
You can overcome the odds of failure by just getting started.

STEP#2   A desire to do business will cost you   pg. #7
Anything you do in life will require some level of finances.
In order to make money in business you have to spend it first.

STEP# 3   Turning ones hobby or passion into business   pg. #9
There's value in your passion, so turn it into profit.
What you take pride in will reflect in your skills-set and expertise.

STEP# 4   Look for ways to produce more business income   pg. #12
Your present talents and skill-set does not put any limits on you.
Your potential earnings increase more when you believe in yourself.

STEP# 5   You're not a carbon copy; you're original   pg. #13
Don't be afraid to do business on your own terms, be innovative.
Entrepreneurs recognize a niche in the market and seize the opportunity.

PAGES 2 LIFE **PUBLISHING**

R L W
Ministries

Business Consultant Booklet Vol. #3

The Study of one's craft is having the access to insight. Now, what will you do with it?

*An in-depth approach to **Examining** the PASSION & **Drive**
Of a True *Entrepreneur* *
By author, *Roderick L. White*

<u>II Timothy 2:15</u> KJV *"Study to show thyself approved unto God, a workman that needeth not be ashamed, rightly dividing the word of truth."*

 One who thrives off energy with a real sense of exuberance to win at all cost has a natural born entrepreneurial spirit. This is something that can't subsequently be taught in a classroom of business or even on a one-on-one mentorship. Either you have that innate ability to go after things, to make it happen for yourself or you just don't. Not to express or promote a negative vibe toward anyone pursuing a business for themselves. But be honest; you know yourself better than anyone. If you have to wait till you have someone telling you it's ok to take a risk or to see the need to make improvements in your approach to business, then you are not an **entrepreneur**. It takes one who has <u>confidence</u> and a real sense of <u>determination</u> to produce something out of nothing.

 NO ONE will hold your hand everyday to initiate the right time to get started. Timing all comes from within you! Once you have evaluated that you're called to create new business, and then run with that opportunity for your chance to win. **(Five Points)** of interest are: Be a WINNER, have CREATIVITY, **eat**, **sleep**, and **breathe** (*business*). There's a purpose for business in you, so you must find it and birth it into existence.

If it hasn't been done; create it! No one can do like you; embrace it. There's some creative genius in you; own it!

<u>Step #1</u>: *Positivity produces good Energy*

> <u>What are the odds of you failing if you never try? 100%</u>! So, if you take the risk to get started there's a good chance you will succeed right? Not guaranteed, but certainly the <u>possibility</u> is <u>greater</u> if you never did start. It's your mindset that produces creativity resulting in successes that manifest the ability to win.

PAGES 2 LIFE **PUBLISHING**

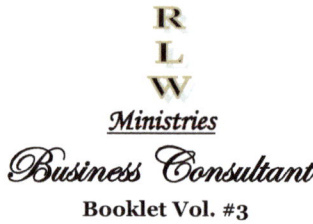

Booklet Vol. #3

Step #1 Continued: *Positivity produces good Energy*

    a. "Knowledge is power," as the old adage states. If you don't have the knowledge or don't understand something then research it, but keep an open positive mindset to learning all about it. The proper structure of a something makes more sense with having an understanding. Even if it seems hard to the task, and you're not sure if you're up to the actual CHALLENGE, don't begin it, with a defeatist attitude. It will cause negative energy to exude from your mental capacity. Don't let anything hinder your ability to acquire the efficient skills to get your business off the ground. Your initiative, drive and future success depend on it.

    b. It's like the old popular children's book approach. *The little engine that could,* **"I think I can, I think I can, I think I can!"**
If you keep pushing it will happen, if you stop now, no one will start it back up for you and your motivation will soon die out. Remember: <u>You're the engine, the cargo and the caboose</u>! What you do now determines what may take place later. Something has to continue to push or drive you from within, fueling your <u>mind</u>, <u>body</u>, and <u>spirit</u>.

    c. Your mindset is the determining factor. If you allow negative thoughts to enter your mind and invade any space there, it will result in some counterproductive consequences. You cannot move forward in progress if you don't believe in your own self and ability. **The most effective tool in achieving something is to make attempts toward your goals regularly, even if the plan of action is not yet perfected**. Some progress of putting thoughts into action is better than not at all. One that has true drive and passion for something with enough effort will ultimately produce a positive and productive result eventually. Feed off those good positive thoughts to obtain a win in the end.

    d. What you consistently hang around or think on as you are trying to accomplish anything, builds with momentum. So as you feed into negative thoughts or subject yourself to negative-minded people, they will suck the life out of any energy you have to put into the task you have at hand. Why cripple your effectiveness, with simple minded thinking or unsupportive people?

PAGES 2 LIFE **PUBLISHING**

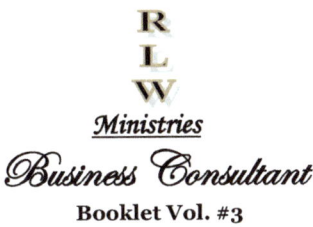

Booklet Vol. #3

Step #1 Continued: *Positivity produces good energy*

    e. You owe yourself a fair opportunity to accomplish your goals. Build upon things that produce a rewarding result and add validation to your plans of action. Any means of productivity causes you to be successful in your efforts. Disassociate yourself from anything that hinders your potential for growth, development and achievement towards becoming an entrepreneur. A positive approach with planning produces good deeds.

Step #2: *A desire to do business will cost you*

Anything you do in life will require some level of finance involved. There's just no way around it. If you want to make money, you will have to spend it first, many financial advisors have stated this even before this booklet. There's should be no surprise; you will have to **count up the cost** first to start a business; <u>evaluate your supplies or products needed</u>, <u>allocate some dollars set aside for startup</u> and <u>strategize a sensible budget</u>. If you plan ahead carefully, pick a target date. Know who are your targeted market and the needs of your customer base. You can make a good first run at opening a business.

    a. <u>What can you do with money available at your exposure</u>? Anything your heart desires, you can achieve on any level and in any location or region you envision for yourself, and no one can stop you. If you have the money you can begin to build a change and transition yourself into controlling your own destiny and future. Why wait, when destiny awaits you now? Whether you're utilizing a piggy bank, mutual funds, savings-checking account, or some personal investment of sorts, you need to start with producing some residual income that builds for yourself in order to be able to create your business in the near future.

PAGES 2 LIFE **PUBLISHING**

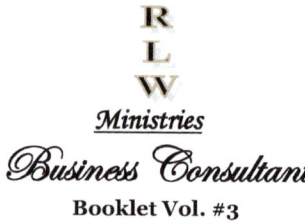

Booklet Vol. #3

Step #2 Continued: *A desire to do business will cost you*

    b. Become business oriented by getting yourself a checking/debit card at an <u>online bank</u> or <u>local banking establishment</u> that you do not touch. Let that account be your business account that you operate out of and of course not do any financial transactions that are not related to business (debits, bills, credits, sales, etc.). Get in the habit of separating business transactions from home expenditures. This is a good business practice for the viability of your organization and will assure your overall success.

    c. **<u>Dos</u> and <u>Don'ts</u>** <u>of considering a start up business are</u>: **Do invest** in your future by getting a location or products you can afford, not what <u>the Jones's</u> have. **Don't get tricked** or caught up by the shiny lights or glamour of already successful businesses, you're not there yet. Give it time and you will grow into improvements. **Do** allow yourself to make savvy investments in presenting a well-thought-out business model. **Don't borrow** any money you don't have the ability to pay back. **Do save** until you have the money to purchase what you need. It will feel better when your needs are accomplished by your own means and you <u>don't owe</u> anyone when it's all said and done. **Don't let anyone** take away your dreams or vision to become an <u>entrepreneur</u>, by the <u>burdens of debits</u>. Be advised; **do your due diligence**, for there are financial challenges ahead, so plan accordingly for those inevitable rainy days. *<u>Set aside any extra funds you possibly can to prepare for lean times</u>.*

    d. Money makes the world go around! There's a proverb that says; "<u>Money is the answer to all things</u>." If you don't understand money you will not be privy to its power to produce wealth and security. I advise listening to some money expertise such as: <u>Suze Orman</u>, <u>Dave Ramsey</u> or even watch the <u>stock market</u>, it all helps, since you're looking to go into business yourself. Possibly pick up a book of some kind, such as *MONEY 101-* <u>The Bible guide for life</u>. All these are vital tools and resources of information to assist you in helping you to succeed in achieving a solid business.

PAGES 2 LIFE **PUBLISHING**

Booklet Vol. #3

<u>*Step #2*</u> *Continued: A desire to do business will cost you*

 e. Starting small is ok; you don't have to have thousands or millions of dollars like one may think to create or start a business. Start where you are, with what you already have: equipment, tools, literature, personal computers, cell phone, etc. It's not necessary to burden yourself with material luxuries that may or may not come right away. It takes sometime even years to obtain better stuff. So keep all of this in mind, but don't stop saving in the process to get there.

 f. Profits will come eventually but don't get discouraged when they are far and few between. <u>That's just business</u> and it works that way. There are many **ups** and **falls** sometimes in daily business. As you may or may not know, the stock market is a prime example of that!

<u>*Step #3*</u>: *Turning ones hobby or passion into business*

<u>What you take pride in doing will show and other's will take notice of your skill and expertise</u>. Your effort will exhibit in your ability to produce good results from all your work. So build on that. You're not just having fun at doing something you love to do; it's more than just another hobby. There's value there, so turn your passion into profit. Begin to think <u>enterprise</u>, its commerce, the opportunity and ability to produce an income for yourself for trade of products and services rendered.

 a. Why is it good to stop looking at your passion as just a hobby? Even if you're doing it out of the kindness of your heart, you have to set some boundaries and start to ask yourself some real hard questions.
<u>Is this charity work I'm doing. and do I intend to keep just doing charity work only? Or is this something that I want to create into a lifelong career and profitable business for myself, since I enjoy it and I'm doing it anyway</u>?

PAGES 2 LIFE **PUBLISHING**

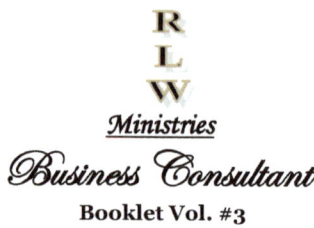

Ministries

Business Consultant

Booklet Vol. #3

Step #3 Continued: *Turning ones hobby or passion into business*

    Ask yourself , <u>do I find myself giving pointers and advice and offering my expertise to others on what to do and how to make things work best for them</u>? If you do, then you are professionally consulting; you have a true business, not just a hobby, but you just need to figure out how to get paid for it! Start charging; it will add value to you work.

b. If you don't start to put value on your work, and your talent and skill set, you will never be taken seriously by others. They will only take advantage of your abilities and what they can get out of you when, and anyway they need it. Don't settle for insignificant means when you can be considered a notable entity yourself. You have something to offer; even though you enjoy doing what you do, don't discount its merit. Just because you find enjoyment in your work doesn't mean you shouldn't be rightfully compensated for producing it. If people truly need your work or service they will pay you for it. *<u>This I will express repeatedly</u>!

<u>People pay for what they value</u>! So put a real **$$** amount on your work and or service. You are not a push over, you are a <u>real resource</u>. Your <u>time</u>, <u>energy</u>, <u>ability</u>, and <u>experience</u> deserves a <u>real</u> **$$** <u>payment</u>.

c. Since consumers in your field of expertise are going to pay for goods or service anyway, why not give them the opportunity to come to you. Doesn't matter if you have competitors near or far who may have more financial reach, you still have something to offer. Monopolize on that personal touch you can offer with a one on one approach. This is what sets you apart from other major players in your field. Don't sell yourself short on gaining any potential business that may come your way.

d. Your next move or decision to go into business for yourself can produce money for you that you didn't have to clock in at another company for. HOW COOL IS THAT? You can potentially be earning really good cash money, as you create and set up your own ligament tax deductible business. <u>Sounds like a good career move to me</u>!

PAGES 2 LIFE **PUBLISHING**

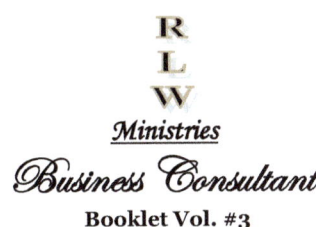

Booklet Vol. #3

Step #3 Continued: *Turning ones hobby or passion into business*

        A taxable business setup is something I explain briefly in "VOL #4 business work booklet," or I can disclose it in full detail within a 30 min. consultation session for an agreed upon fee, see page 28. Example: that's a business module!

e. The tools, skills set, and abilities you possess are all given to you innately to be used to their full potential, so MAXIMIZE on that! Once you've discovered you're good at something, and you find pleasure in doing it, begin to invest into it. In order to make money with something you have to spend money on it first as I've stated before.
Example: Acquire tools, supplies, literature, equipment, merchandise, etc. All this makes your business a valuable resource in the market place for consumers to tap into. If there are no products or services to offer, there's no business to render or any means to produce any income. Use common sense to produce **dollars** and **cents**.

f. Quick reminder: **STOP** doing favors for people that don't appreciate your hard work. They're just taking advantage of your skill and generosity. Unless it's charitable; again, it needs to be profitable. You deserve to get PAID for what others require from you, your talents, time and skill set. If you make people pay for your time or products and services, they will appreciate your abilities more.

g. You're not a shade-tree mechanic sort to speak, so stop acting like one. Even if you didn't get formerly trained at some trade school or acquire a degree at some university for your level of expertise, you still are worth your time and effort. Make sure you charge for your goods and services. If they seriously need your help they'll cough up the cash. TRUST ME; if they really want to do business, **they will pay you**!

PAGES 2 LIFE **PUBLISHING**

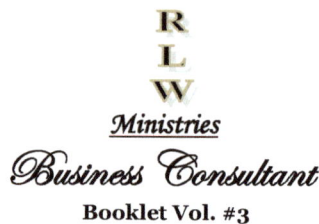

Booklet Vol. #3

Step #4: *Look for ways to produce more business income*

Your present talent and skill set do not put any limits on you. Nor does your current business determine that you only have the ability or potential to produce a minimum amount of newly earned dollars. Increase in your earning potential is a direct result of you believing in your own success. As you push for more, more income will follow. Don't just settle for little, when you can have so much more to look forward to. You can obtain more clients, more exposure, and produce more dollars, it's all very possible!

a. Ask yourself, if you are satisfied with the income you're bringing in so far. If not, than you need to expand your products or services or maybe both. It's possible you could be limiting your profitability all because you have not thought big enough or hard enough on potential earnings. What do you got to lose on expansion? Think on it, if you don't restructure earning potential with expanding, you will stay at the same income level. Even if you hire others to help you, at some point, you still have to offer more as a service or product to obtain more money.

b. Don't get too comfortable at bringing in minimum amount of dollars even when the money comes at a steady flow of business. You can always do more if you strive to produce more through creative means. *Possibly do a survey of ideas by asking your regular or potential customers if they are in the market for additional services. If so, try to meet the demands by implementing those services if it's doable.

c. New services and new products can complement something you already offer. Why let those potential $$ dollars walk away from you? If an idea comes to mind, try to add it to your existing business. That idea maybe your next window to a successful prosperous business for you ahead.

PAGES 2 LIFE **PUBLISHING**

Ministries

Business Consultant

Booklet Vol. #3

Step #4 Continued: *Look for ways to produce more business income*

    d. Offering multiple services or relatable goods make multiple streams of income possible. As the movie line says, show me the MONEY!!! Wasted ideas and dreams result in lost earnings and future profits. In the business world, you have to keep hustling, and stay on your grind.

    e. You have got try to outsmart or out shine your competitors to thrive and survive. Maximize on all available opportunities to gain more income and retain those dollars for the future. All phases of business are not profitable. There will surely be some lean times as well, ahead. So prepare for those lean times by coming up with a different strategy to make money.
Example: If you have a business as a lawn and brush cutter during (spring and summer) months, become a tree pruner and snow shovel serviceman during (fall and winter) months. *Add to your current services or flip the inventory to seasonal products. Create that sense of flexibility through a limited supply in high demand!

    f. "No money should be left on the table," as the saying goes. Gain those crumbs off the table in **cents** if you will. What others will not pickup off the table because it maybe small dollars to them. Just think, the more small dollars you can add to the pot, the more profit you will add to your bank account and the more your income will increase. Makes a lot of **sense** right?

Step #5: *You're not a carbon copy you're original*

    What you're offering is exclusive, so act accordingly. Make your clients and customers think they can't get the services and products you offer anywhere else better. Your fair prices, and services and products should feel like a one-stop shop for them.

PAGES 2 LIFE **PUBLISHING**

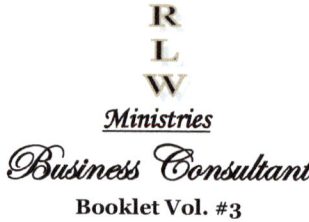

Ministries

Business Consultant

Booklet Vol. #3

<u>*Step #5*</u> *Continued: You're not a carbon copy you're original*

a. Bank on your customers wanting to only do business with you, all because they are treated so well. You've pride yourself on building a new business that pays very close attention to detail. You offer that special hands-on approach as well as your ability to deliver good results. That will keep customers coming back many times over. All of these traits stand out and renders a good recommendation for you.

b. What makes you stand out is your professionalism, courtesy, warming inviting personality, and your willingness to accommodate any potential business or returning customers that come your way. Most people recognize their first impression or encounter of dealing with you. To quote a co-employee of mine, "**<u>You never get a second chance to make a first impression</u>**."So make it a good lasting one!

c. Don't be afraid to do business on your own terms; what works for others may not be the norm for you. Do you, it's natural. Go with that vibe of what feels comfortable not what everyone else is doing. <u>Originality is key</u>, your business does not have to be categorized or classified like everyone else's. You have to be noticeable and desirable but not fake in what you offer your clients or customers. If you say you can deliver on some service or product, <u>PLEASE DO SO</u>! It will save your business from so many losses and possible bad reputation.

d. <u>Produce well,</u> <u>be innovative,</u> <u>explore improvements</u>, and do your best to <u>accommodate regularly</u>. Always <u>render quality work</u>, good <u>products</u> and <u>great customer service</u> which go a long way. All of these good traits will equal a beneficial and promising productive business for many years to come. * Remember: No COOKIE-cutter business!

e. An **effective entrepreneur:** sees a <u>niche in the market</u> and monopolizes on the opportunity by realizing that they are equipped to fill it, and so they diligently pursue it and get it done. Be that <u>go-getter</u>, not the <u>one that regretted</u> letting the chance pass by. Don't be one who misses that opportunity by not getting up and making it happen.

Ministries
Business Consultant

RLW Ministries: Guide to; product placement, capital investing, and market analysis is an added service that is not provided in this entrepreneur's booklet. *But, I can offer guidance for an agreed consultant's fee **session**. On my website below those consultation sessions are offered as a service to get your new business going and running strong.

Volume #3 A True Entrepreneur's booklet has all the info you need to get your new business successfully off the ground. Upon finishing it, I have also provided **Volume #4** A Good Businessman booklet available as an added bonus. It'll help you facilitate your journey and new career as a successful entrepreneur and now also as a prominent business owner.

*I've been fortunately blessed to launch two successful businesses while also publishing three great books. The books are a Christian trilogy on **Purposed & Divine**. So professionally, I've extended my business expertise and services to help others become entrepreneurs and great businessman too. You can find me on AMAZON or Barnes & Noble or at RoderickLWhiteministries.com*

Ministries
Business Consultant Booklet Vol. #3

I highly look forward to further being of service to you with any of your business needs. For any services and consultation sessions, feel free to contact me via email @ rodwhitepastor1@icloud.com

731.326.0641
Roderick L. White Ministries
P.O. Box 10142
Jackson, TN. 38308

RLW Ministries: *I'm excited about your journey as a new entrepreneur, so you can only imagine what your bright future holds for you as an established businessman. I wish above all, that you flourish, excel, and become prosperous in all you do as you share your products and services with the world. May God continue to bless your journey and direct your awesome talent and skill to create new business!*

PAGES 2 LIFE **PUBLISHING**

R
L
W

Ministries

Business Consultant

Booklet Vol. #4

THE STRATEGY

Exhibiting The **STAMINA** & Mentality Of A Good Businessman

PAGES 2 LIFE **PUBLISHING**

R L W
Ministries
Business Consultant

Booklet Vol. #4

THE STRATEGY

Exhibiting the STAMINA *& Mentality of a Good Businessman* VOL. #4

TABLE OF CONTENTS *continued*

STEP#1   **A diamond in the rough**   pg. #19
    Don't let anyone kill your pride or steal your success!
    Your ideas may be buried temporarily, but they are worth their
    weight in gold. Your effort to dig deep into business builds character.

STEP#2   **Know your mode of operation**   pg. #21
    Establishing consistency in set-up of a business is the key.
    But, to conduct business successfully, you have to decide on a locale.

STEP# 3   **Appearances and impressions are everything**   pg. #23
    People's first impression of you or your business can make or break
    your ability to sell, and gain a customer base.

STEP# 4   **New deals promote new customers**   pg. #24
    Become creative and innovative in producing new sales. People love
    sales, and everyone likes a good deal. So more DEALS= More Sells!

STEP# 5   **Expanding your brand by increasing your reach**   pg. #26
    In order to make your brand more profitable, you have to expand
    your product and services somehow. Expansion= Added Distribution!

PAGES 2 LIFE **PUBLISHING**

Ministries

Business Consultant Booklet Vol. #4

You created and birthed this new business; Now, how will you make it profitable?

An insightful look into the challenges and complexities of what it takes to acquire the true acumen of a good businessman

By, author -*Roderick L. White*

<u>Luke 14:28</u> KJV "*For which of you, intending to build a tower, sitteth not down first, and counteth the cost, whether he have sufficient to finish it?*"

Any person with enough effort can achieve the desired results of opening their own business, but it takes one with many necessary traits to be productive at keeping the business running successfully. Your heart, passion, drive, stamina and positive mindset with a sense of practicality is the formula that makes it all work in your favor. But more importantly, <u>long years of hard work</u> + <u>diligence</u> + <u>great service</u> and or <u>good products</u> = long-lasting positive results. No pain, no gain, no business, and **no money**-producing income. You have to work hard to become successful and to stay in business for years to come. **Longevity in business depends upon one's mentality**. So, is creating business your life, or are you waiting for the next brainy idea? What you create, birth, and then nurture produces a promising offspring. So if you planted the seeds and watered that business, it will sooner or later produce a fruitful vine.

What other's dared to attempt, you did it. What seemed to be insignificant, you accomplished it with greatness!

<u>Step #1</u>: *A diamond in the rough*

<u>Don't let anyone kill your pride or steal your success</u>! Your ideas maybe buried temporarily but they are worth their weight in gold. Through trial, test, and error, you will soon shine and sparkle; your day is coming. Hang in there with your ideas, brain storms, and creativity; they all have merit and value. It's your personal responsibility to dust off all the debris, and dirt that tried to bury and devalue you. <u>You're blossoming now</u>!

PAGES 2 LIFE **PUBLISHING**

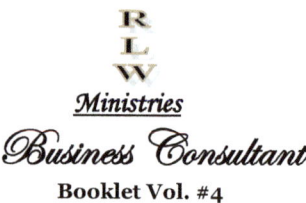

Booklet Vol. #4

Step #1 Continued: *A diamond in the rough*

a. It's time for your business ideas to see the light of day. So unearth all those talents, skills, natural ability, and creativity you possess that will ultimately make your business unique and stand out from others. Innately you have what it take to become a vibrant businessman. Take ownership of your God given gift to create something significant out of nothing; your creative ideas already have worth. You're now becoming productive with the business you created from your own hands and ability, so give a chance to grow and develop under your care. Know that there's value in what you're selling and offering as a service to others. You just got to trust your ability and the process that consequently will lead you to success.

b. Sometimes the hardest materials are the most valuable after all. Often the roughest and toughest substances are the most durable and will exhibit longevity and endurance for many years to come. You may blossom like a flower but you must develop and mature tough as a tree or even as a stern cactus that's rooted deep in the hard dry dirt just to survive. You must have a strong conviction in your belief that your business will not only grow and succeed but it will last for a very long time. So dig your heels into all you got and find out what your business venture can ultimately become. Your efforts may be tested and tried, but you can still prevail and blossom with enough perseverance and determination.

c. If you want to eliminate your own doubts, fears, and your existing insufficiencies, and even do better than your competitors, you have to work hard to overcome it all. It may seem too hard to do that at times, but it's worth every penny in the end. If you hang in there until something turns favorable for you or somehow becomes hopeful, it may prove to be your time and chance to truly prosper. Don't give up on any struggle or challenges; give your business time to blossom and develop into a great reward for you to enjoy someday. GREATNESS comes to those that PERSEVERE, but also those who patiently WAIT!

PAGES 2 LIFE **PUBLISHING**

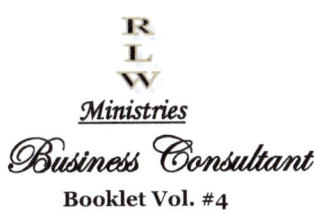

Ministries

Business Consultant

Booklet Vol. #4

Step #1 Continued: *A diamond in the rough*

    d. "**Rome wasn't built in a day**," as the saying goes. So <u>patience</u>, <u>dedication</u>, <u>endurance</u>, <u>drive</u>, and enough <u>due diligence</u> will get you to a desired finish. It will result in a business you can truly be proud of for many years to come. Marvel at what you can potentially become not what you necessarily have now. It's a building process not an overnight sensation of some kind. You're investing in a bright future that will produce a good flow of continuous business, not just for right NOW!

    e. <u>Sometimes your ideas and business ventures have to stay on the potter's wheel for a bit, in order to be perfected</u>. But that doesn't mean those ideas are not useable or doable. What may start off slow in the process will build and has merit and value accredited to you, taking the necessary time and effort to produce a display of productivity and excellence. If done right, your intentions and effort will result in a well-thought-out plan of action to build a successful business, which ultimately produces much wealth. <u>Those dirty hands build character</u>!

Step #2: *Know your mode of operation*

    In order to set up any particular business, first you must decide on your location for which you will run your business from or out of, and then proceed with details on setup. Secondly get a good sense of potential traffic flow from surrounding businesses or similar businesses by taking into account who maybe your target customer base. Will your business be a standard <u>brick and mortar</u> location, <u>truck or car transport service</u>, <u>home delivery service</u>, or some type of <u>mobile food truck</u>, or maybe a web based <u>online service</u>? Or is it some type of venue <u>hosting service</u>, etc? Example: speaking engagements, equipment setup for party occasions, marketing and advertising service, or some type of consultant service, *<u>Establishing consistency is the key</u>!

PAGES 2 LIFE **PUBLISHING**

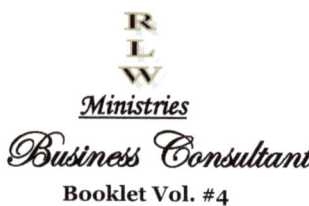

Booklet Vol. #4

Step #2 Continued: *Know your mode of operation*

    a. The determining factor for setting up and conducting a successful business is to establish a point of sale (POS) to take in payments. If there's no ability to receive payments, or charge any customers for products or services you cannot conduct business. The methods for which you take in payments have to be financially secure means and easily accessible to you and your customers or clients. If there are any discrepancies in payment methods, it may cost you revenue or even cause you to lose that customer permanently.

    b. There are many modes or methods of taking in payments. You must decide on what is most suitable for your type of business. As you look at the modern ways of taking payments, don't rule out any methods until you have set up your business **POS** system properly. Multiple payments methods may invite new customer base. You have several sources of payment methods that are available for you to utilize. To name a few: **Cash registers** with debit/**credit** features, **Pay Pal-Here** Chip and Tap readers, Square POS, and even invoice billing.

    c. As you're factoring in all the required things for setting up your business, consider if you want it to be at a physical location and make sure it's a good visible one from the street. If you're out of sight, your business is definitely out of mind. As the saying goes, **location, location. location!!!** *You want your business to be successful, so people also have to have adequate parking or your business has to be within walking distance from the street near a parking structure. This careful consideration will assure they will patronize your physical place of business. If not, they will go elsewhere. Establishing an easily accessible business for your customer base is utmost important.

    d. If your business is a mobile one or online-based, you still have to be considerate of accessibility. If people can't locate your business or have trouble navigating your site; it can stunt your growth potential. Do all you can to make your business reachable to all markets and noticeable by all demographics as possible. Technology is your friend, **USE IT!** Example: Google, Bling, **Amazon** Alexa, and Yelp use them all!

PAGES 2 LIFE **PUBLISHING**

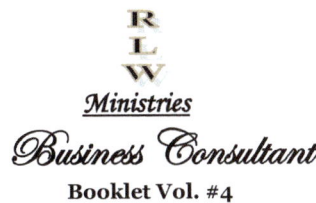

Ministries

Business Consultant

Booklet Vol. #4

Step #3: Appearances and impressions are everything

People are drawn to what looks good. Their first impression of what you're offering will grow or kill your business. If it looks homemade and not professional, you are only hurting your potential to grow a good customer base. Make sure you pay much attention to detail as you properly name your business. Your decor or online graphic design has to appeal to all business markets, **local, national** and **even abroad**. If you think professionally, you will become BIG and successful.

a. What kind of impression do you want to leave on your new customers as they visit your place of business? Whether it's a physical location or online shop you have one shot to give off the right vibes? People will always remember their first experience of how well put together your place of business is on their initial attempt to patronize. If you disappoint them in appearing unprofessional or unorganized it will reflect in you obtaining any potential sales. Take every opportunity to make a good impression on customers who visit your business. If you don't it can possibly leave a wrong or bad impression on visitors.

b. Word of mouth can be your greatest asset or possibly your greatest downfall. If people have a good experience with you, they will surely recommend you to their family, associates, and friends and even to strangers they happen to meet in casual conversation. On the other hand, if people have a bad experience with your business, they may possibly bad-mouth your business as well. It's totally up to you as a **good business owner**, to do all you can to not let bad experiences happen. In all cases, try your best to alleviate any potential bad experiences with all customers in doing that, offer **excellent customer service** all of the time. Be cordial and always inviting!

c. A warm atmosphere will create wonders for your business and invite customers to return in the future to purchase products and services. Ask yourself, does my business appeal to the general public? If I were a customer and not the owner, would I patronize this business, yes/no?

PAGES 2 LIFE **PUBLISHING**

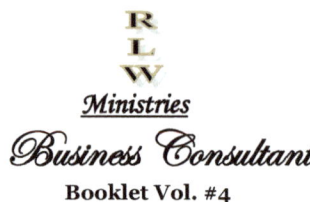

Booklet Vol. #4

Step #3 Continued: *Appearances and impressions are everything*

    d. Your physical appearance plays a distinct and major part in whether you're considered a professional establishment or not. It doesn't matter what type of business you are conducting, you must maintain a professional persona always. Whether you're in a suit and tie or not or in blue jeans and a work shirt and boots, your attire matters.
Let your business LOGO & Name stand out and get good attention

    e. Example: All uniforms should have business name embroidered or printed on them. You should customize and print your business name on all polo's and t-shirts with company's logo. Even more so, if you're utilizing an automobile for business services you need to have all vehicles with company logo printed on them as well. If your car or truck is used personally and professionally, **vehicle magnetic banners**; are a good idea for multiple usages. It all shows uniformity and organization for conducting a professional and soundly structured business operation.

    f. What you show people related to your business advertises what you offer. So keep that in mind as you look to build an effective and productive business with longevity. Perception and appearance also builds a reputation for the way you conduct yourself as a professional or not. The old saying goes: "If it quacks like a duck, looks like a duck, walks like a duck; it's probably a DUCK!" So only advertise what you want people to see and think about your established business nothing more or less. You're the face of the business, so present it well, but know your location also because that is what builds an established landmark.

Step #4: New deals promote new customers

    Become creative and innovative in producing more sales. You have to find ways to continue to increase your income-earning potential. Be consistent in price but generous in promotions. People love sales, and that's just the truth. Deals+Deals=**Sales**!

PAGES 2 LIFE **PUBLISHING**

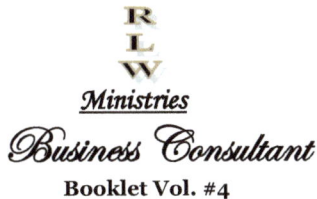

Ministries

Business Consultant

Booklet Vol. #4

Step #4 Continued: New deals promote new customers

    a. What you offered last week or even last month may stay at the same prices but occasionally think about implementing temporary sales to beef up your traffic to your physical location or online site. Offering big **sales**, exclusive **deals** and ad **promotions**: are the ABCs of producing more sells by advertising your business services and products at a lower cost. The more people feel like they are saving a dollar, the more they will spend even more dollars.

    b. Some general tricks of the trade are to promote prices that appear to be lower in cost not to deceive customers but to achieve new sales. Some examples are **$10.99** and **$15.49**. Sounds a lot lower in cost than $11.00 and $15.50, even though they are both close in price point. It's **retail 101**; psychologically, the brain thinks it's getting a much better deal. Seems simple enough in theory, but that's what gets the job done or invites traffic into your doors, causing customers to steadily continue to come back time and again.

    c. If you see that you have a certain customer that loves doing business with you regularly, there's nothing wrong with offering them additional savings or exclusive one-time deals. Even if they are a first time customer, you might want to offer some incentives to earn their future business. Giving an extra 10% or 20% off at the point of sale goes a very long with new customers and existing ones thereby building a rapport as you're acquiring a longtime trusted patriot to frequent your place of business.

    d. There's nothing like seeing a new face in your place of business. Find out what led them there, and try your best to win them over as a regular customer. Don't be so hard on your prices that you lose the opportunity to render your products and services at a temporary discount. Of course, your prices have to have some consistency, or you will look unstructured and deceptive. But the objective of sales promotions is to occasionally offer more deals on normal-priced products and services to increase more continued traffic flow.

PAGES 2 LIFE **PUBLISHING**

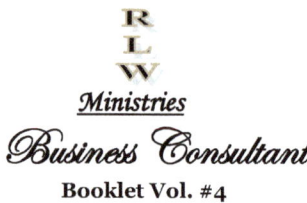

Ministries

Business Consultant

Booklet Vol. #4

Step #4 Continued: *New deals promote new customers*

    e. Every customer needs to feel wanted and appreciated! If they feel like they're getting something that no one else is offered, they will certainly come back again. As a business owner, put yourself in a customer's shoes.

    f. <u>Ask yourself</u>: Did the customer feel like you took all of their money, or do they feel that they saved some money when the sale was final by doing business with you rather than some competitor? <u>This speaks VOLUMES</u>! Nobody likes to feel like they were taken advantage of, but everyone wants to feel like they were taken care of. Simple enough, but courtesy in retail is common sense and in life in general.

Step #5: *Expanding your brand by increasing your reach*

How one increases their ability to reach multiple markets is how they consider taking their brand to the next level. <u>This requires a businessman with some level of self-confidence or willingness to take a risk</u>. In order to make your brand more desirable and profitable, you must expand in some way or another, whether it's adding to your products and services or setting up additional locations. Going regional or national may require you to implement fulfilling online sales orders to ship outside your single business location. <u>Expansion=Distribution</u>.

    a. If you're a sole proprietor or still even a mom-and- pop type operation but successful at what you already do, don't be limited in your earning potential and ability to create exposure to new customers by not becoming versatile in your ability to sell. Tunnel vision in business can often cut off your peripheral perspective on the bigger picture, which is to gain more sales as time and years progress. PLAN TO EXPAND!

    b. There should always be some short-term goals in mind as you continue to do business on a regular basis. One should consider where they want to be at from **LYTD** vs.**YTD** sales= (<u>last year's</u> vs. <u>this year's</u>) **Growth**!

PAGES 2 LIFE **PUBLISHING**

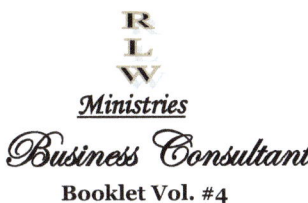

Ministries

Business Consultant

Booklet Vol. #4

Step #5 Continued: *Expanding your brand by increasing your reach*

    c. Just as you're putting attention on short term goals, **long-term goals** are just as crucial and productive to progress your business to the next level of trading. There is always room for improvement, so continue to push yourself to acquire more customers and achieve more exposure. If your business only profited **$40K** each year for the first **five years** of operating you can earn even better than that. Make sure you shoot for **$50K** or more for the next five years. If you become aggressive enough, and creative in reaching more markets your brand and business volume will surely grow and expand each year with the right amount time and effort.

    d. All national and global brands started small, but the key aspect is they didn't stay small, they GREW. If you think only with a mom-and- pop type mentality, you will stunt your future business growth every time. The business world is changing constantly so in order to continue with producing a successful business, know that you have to adjust with the ever-changing market. Any type of business that hopes to keep doing business successfully has the obligation and responsibility to be marketable at all cost. This is done by staying current, relevant, and easily accessible in order to be profitable in all possible markets. Your business has the ability to be diverse as it gets people's ATTENTION!!!

    e. What you did last year to advertise, or to promote and gain exposure, do more of that, or research what works and what gains even more exposure. There are no limits to how profitable your business can become; there's no stopping point into which you can become noticed. As you utilize the resources and opportunities that are allotted to you, you will become another success story. When expansion opportunity knocks, it would be unwise as a businessman to not open the DOOR!

    f. Your next investment to expand your business could make you RICH! Examples: **AMAZON**, Google, **APPLE**, Microsoft, and **Face** book, etc. The list just goes on and on for endless possibilities to become a global branded business yourself. You can achieve multiple millions in cash earning potential, through expansion, if you so desire, it can HAPPEN!

PAGES 2 LIFE **PUBLISHING**

Ministries
Business Consultant

RLW Ministries: Guide to product placement, capital investing, and market analysis is an added service that is not provided in this entrepreneur's booklet. *But, I can offer guidance for an agreed consultant's fee **session**. On my website below those consultation sessions are offered as a service to get your new business going and running strong.

The **Volume #3** A True Entrepreneur's booklet has all the info you need to get your new business successfully off the ground. Upon finishing it, I have also provided **Volume #4** A Good Businessman booklet. It's available as an added bonus to help you facilitate your journey and new career as a successful entrepreneur and now also as a prominent business owner.

*I've been fortunately blessed to launch two successful businesses while also publishing three great books. The books are a Christian trilogy on **Purposed & Divine**. So professionally, I've extended my business expertise and services to help others become entrepreneurs and great businessman too. You can find me on AMAZON or Barnes & Noble or at RoderickLWhiteministries.com*

Ministries
Business Consultant Booklet Vol. #4

I highly look forward to further being of service to you with any of your business needs. For any services and consultation sessions, feel free to contact me via email @ **rodwhitepastor1@icloud.com**
731.326.0641
Roderick L. White Ministries
P.O. Box 10142
Jackson, TN. 38308

RLW Ministries: I'm excited about your journey as a new entrepreneur, so you can only imagine what your bright future holds for you as an established good businessman. I wish above all, that you flourish, excel, and become prosperous in all you do as you share your products and services with the world. May God continue to bless your journey and direct your awesome talent and skill to create new business!

PAGES 2 LIFE **PUBLISHING**

Ministries

Writer's Consultant & Business Consultant

Est. 2020

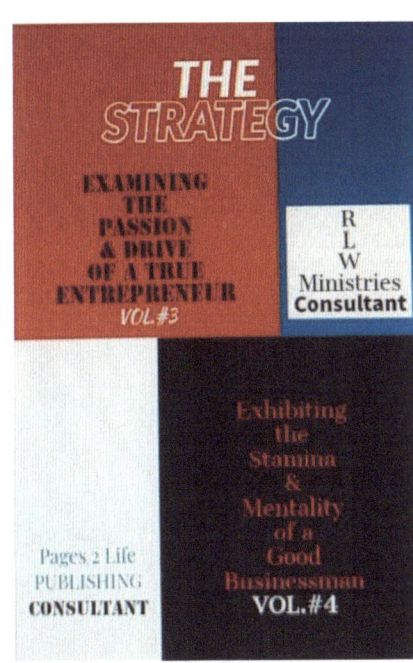

Est. 2020

RoderickLWhiteMinistries.com

Est. 2017 copyright, all registered and catalogued @ The Library of Congress 2017-2021

www.ingramcontent.com/pod-product-compliance
Lightning Source LLC
Chambersburg PA
CBHW040348220526
45473CB00009B/2817